Praise

"Take one quote before bed-time. You'll wake up
refreshed and revitalized."

—MARTIN RUTTE,
co-author of *Chicken Soup For The Soul At Work*

"Everyone will find some helpful insight in this book.
Take the words to heart that enlighten and inspire
you and skip what doesn't."

—BERNIE SIEGEL, MD,
author of *Prescriptions For Living* and
365 Prescriptions For The Soul

"Many parts of a successful life are simple—but not
easy! Rob and Russ do a wonderful job of reminding
us to do what we know is the right thing."

—MARSHALL GOLDSMITH,
recognized by the American Management Association
as one of the 50 great thinkers and leaders who
have impacted the field of management

"Give this book to yourself and every employee as a gift for inspiring effective change!"

—KRAIG KRAMERS,
CEO, Speaker and author of *CEO Tools...the Nuts-n-Bolts of Business for Every Manager's Success*, and management coach

"Reading *That Was Zen, This Is Wow* is like having a warm chat over hot coffee with your most knowledgeable mentor. The wise aphorisms in this book float elegantly off the page, and at least several dozen of them slapped me into full recognition of my faults. I couldn't be more thankful."

—BEN MCCONNELL,
co-author of *Creating Customer Evangelists: How Loyal Customers Become a Volunteer Sales Force*

"This book may just be the key to unlock the potential for success we all have within."

—HARRY PAUL,
co-author, *FISH! A Remarkable Way to Boost Morale and Improve Results*

"In a world that moves too fast, overloads us with options, information, and useless data, every now and then we need to pause, breathe, and relax. *That Was Zen, This Is Wow* is the perfect antidote. Grab the book, turn to any page, pick one item, read it, and put it into action. Repeat as needed. It's just what the doctor ordered!"

—LESLIE CHARLES,
author of *Why Is Everyone So Cranky?* and *All Is Not Lost*

"*That Was Zen, This Is Wow* is about seizing the moment and doing what you know in your heart is the right thing to do. Some great gems to get you motivated."

—ROBERT FRANKEN,
author of *Human Motivation*

"Here is a treasure of simple truths. Five of these truths are found in the biographies of every successful person."

—Dennis Kleper,
entrepreneur, educator and advocate

"An inspirational read and perfect use for all levels of an organization–inspiration for everyone."

—John Z. Ferguson,
SVP, Sales Americas, Getty Images

"People on the move will take this book with them."

—Jeannette Seibly,
author of *Hiring Amazing Employees*

"In business, little things often produce big results. *That Was Zen…* is a 'big book' with 'big ideas' packed in little capsules of wisdom."

—Rod Johnson,
TEC Chair

That Was Zen, This Is Wow

232 Ideas for Transforming Your Life
from Ordinary to Extraordinary

By

Robert S. Engelman III & Russell J. Riendeau, PhD

Eyecatcher Press

ISBN 0-9654631-2-5

Cover and interior design by The Pepper Group, Palatine, Illinois

Printed by Press Tech, Des Plaines, Illinois

To order additional copies of this book, please call
847-945-7573 or 847-381-0977.

Eyecatcher Press

PO Box 1303, Barrington, Illinois 60010

Printed in United States of America

10 9 8 7 6 5 4 3 2 1

Acknowledgements

From Rob:

Laughter, smiles and happiness are noble words to live by, but they mean very little if you cannot share them with others. To all of you who have provided emotional, physical, spiritual, and social support over the years...*thank you!* Without you, none of this would be possible. A special acknowledgement goes out to my "Who Wants to Be a Millionaire" lifelines...

Stephanie Engelman - You have been the best "best friend," wife, inspiration, lover, mother, I could have ever imagined. Your determination, drive, and ability to love my "shtick" is beyond belief. When life turns upside down remember these two things...breathe in, breathe out.

Hillary Engelman - Your beauty, honesty, and compassion oozes out of your pores, and warms every room you step in. Whether I am near or far, always remember that I will be your boat driver.

Eli Engelman - There has never been a boy with a heartier, more contagious laugh than you–it is just one of the reasons why you are the person that you are. Let's go outside and play catch.

From Russ:

A book of this nature is never born on an island of one or two minds. Inspiration and insight often come from quiet people with interesting insights to the human condition. Special thanks to:

Cheryl Riendeau - On your impressions as to what is right, I would bet the farm.

Danielle and Grant - Thanks for questioning everything.

Jim Murphy - Your insights to this project–in the Starbucks on Rt. 14–was well worth the cost of the Hazelnut Latte.

John Cywinski - Your belief in the value of this book kept me committed.

Our TEC colleagues - Your candid feedback was invaluable.

The Pepper Group - Your creativity and urgency was what we needed.

Other books by Russell Riendeau

Thinking on Your Seat: A Catalyst to Create Respect, Results & Revenue (For the Recruiting Professional)

Finders Keepers: Attracting & Retaining Top Sales Professionals

The Insider's Guide to Getting Great Job Offers (co-author Brady Spencer)

Introduction

*"To make a difference, you have to
make something happen."*

This a book for busy people. That is why it is short.
That's why the ideas are immediately implementable.
That's why we use humor, emotion and visual images
to encourage recall and retention. This is also a book for
people that want to make a difference—whatever "making
a difference" means to you.

In today's ever-changing business and social landscapes,
we sometimes forget to share powerful ideas and
knowledge in a meaningful and relevant manner—or
worse, we sometimes forget to listen when a great idea
comes along. We wrote this book mindful that your time
and attention are being tugged from many directions.
Thus, the content is designed to be simple yet thought-
provoking. After reading, you will immediately be
motivated to create successes in your daily events, be
it in actions or thoughts. From this point forward,
your "now" can be "WOW."

So, in the spirit of brevity, here are three additional
points worthy of space:

First, "Zen" and "Wow" are simply metaphors, or
symbols, that represent unique ways for you to see and

experience opportunities and challenges in everyday events. Metaphors are also proven tools to aid recall and retention of new learning and behaviors. (We like using the purple elephant metaphor, as one example, to describe opportunities and challenges.)

Secondly, *That was Zen* was created as a fun philosophy to guide you towards both intrinsic and extrinsic success.

Finally, *That was Zen* is a work in progress. Research in motivation theory, psychology, sociology and best practices in business have shown even slight changes in behavior, thought processes and communication skills are effective ways to excel in your personal and professional lives. People have even told us this book invites more than one reading, as with subsequent reads you'll find new ideas you missed the first go around.

We'd encourage you to write your own version of *Zen to Wow*. Pick a topic, a passion, or a challenge you feel strongly about and share your knowledge with the community.

Zen is about choice and self-knowledge. Wow is the courageous journey to empowerment and an accountable life.

Enjoy the journey.

It's 3 a.m.—where is your mind? That's the issue that deserves your attention and action.

1

Everybody is a "Free Agent"
regardless of who your business
card says you work for.

2

Achievement Theory 6/12: what
you decide to do between 6 P.M. and
midnight is what will change your
life for the better.

3

Discipline test: Next time you drive
past a police car shooting radar, don't
look back in the rear view mirror.

4

"Is what I'm *about* to do going to take me closer to or further from my goal?" (A great question to ask yourself 25 times a day.)

5

The good witch, Glinda, in *The Wizard of Oz,* would have been blacklisted if she were a management consultant. Not telling Dorothy she could have solved her logistics problem anytime by just tapping her heels three times was nasty. Give accurate data.

14

6

A good question builds credibility better than a good answer. Prepare well.

7

Most people do their *best* work
when they're *not* working. Take
your vacation days.

8

If talk of cutbacks is in the air,
find ways to become more visible and
valuable ASAP. Become, in the
altered words of Robert Palmer's
tune: *Simply Indispensable.*

15

9

The law of averages eventually
shows up, but play hard anyway...
in case it's late.

10

Never negotiate with a plumber
on Superbowl Sunday. Pick
your spots to deal.

11

A job without a high degree of
accountability will never pay
you what you demand.

16

12

Optimism is always a better choice.

13

Patriotism is always in style.

14

We all put our pants on the same way:
one *arm* at a time. Respect and embrace
diverse ideas and opinions.

15

The most productive thing at the
moment *could be* a nap.

17

16

Never, never, never, never,
never discuss compensation on
a first interview. Never.

17

Reread the one above.

18

First consider the other person's
point-of-view...you.

19

Wrestle your purple elephants
(your primary challenges) to
the ground when they're
small. Elephants grow
bigger, you know.

18

20

Personal fitness can't be stored. It is an
ongoing process built into daily habits.

21

Every person you meet from this day on
can change your life. How will you
change someone's life today?

22

You always have another choice in
any given situation. Always.

23

Do the expected (what's right)
unexpectedly and experience
great results.

24

Time standing in line to buy the 40
million dollar lottery ticket is better used
making another sales call, organizing your
next day or studying laws of success.
This "time" is the odds-on favorite
to make more money.

25

Philanthropy is not a privilege of the
wealthy. Start a worthwhile
foundation of your own
on a small scale.

26

To make a difference, you have to
make something happen.

20

27

Earning an MBA won't
necessarily make you smarter,
but it makes others *think* you
are. This buys you time
to figure things out.

28

If you're not reading something
thirty minutes a day, you're
falling way behind.

29

The schoolyard bully rarely ice skates
very well. Arrange to meet him on your
frozen turf. Pick your battles wisely.

30

There's a reason your umbilical
cord doesn't have a plug at
the end: you're designed to
run on your own battery.

22

31

We all have genius within us
in some capacity. Look for it
in others and yourself.

32

Sales people will expend more effort in a
30-day contest for a $150 portable TV
than they will in their day-to-day job for
an extra $2000 in their paycheck at the
end of the quarter. Some behaviors are
driven by short-term incentives.

23

33

Always tell the Emperor when he or she
is naked. They'll thank you for it.

34

Always pull over for the fire truck—they may be heading to your house!

35

The guy riding your bumper in morning traffic may be the customer you're traveling to meet.

36

No need to open your windows in the event of a tornado. A tornado's perfectly capable of opening your windows on its own.

—Revised folk wisdom

37

The only difference between you
and a millionaire is money.

38

Before making a presentation to a
group, make friends with a few
in the front and back to have
friendly eyeballs to find.

39

Keep your camera ready at all times.

40

Be the first Dunk Tank volunteer
at the company picnic.

41

And never be "the arm" that sinks the
boss if she volunteers before you.

26

42

THINK.

43

Don't think too much.

44

Passions trump goals.

45

Some hobbies should remain so.

46

Always ascertain the presence of
toilet paper before commencing.

27

47

The day you're no longer willing to
tolerate something is a glorious day.
That day is your epiphany.

48

Don't sneeze into the hand
you shake with.

49

Before a meeting with the boss, picture
him or her in one of those hospital
gowns going for an x-ray. Not so
tough looking anymore, eh?

28

50

Always accept water or a soft drink in an
interview. It breaks the ice and is
symbolic of eating and drinking
with friends. People rarely eat
and drink with the enemy.

51

All it takes is 21 *days* to break
a habit. Sometimes, all it takes is 21
years to pick the right day to
begin. Pick today.

52

People associate change with giving
something up. Not true. *Non-change*
gives up our opportunity to experience
something new.

53

When people ask for career advice don't give it. Ask them questions about what they want, and they'll find their way more quickly.

54

Entrepreneurs would rather work 80 hours a week for themselves instead of 40 hours for someone else. Are you ready?

55

Over 75% of graduates are in a totally different field ten years after graduating college. Just complete your degree.

30

56

Once you resign from your job be
prepared for your peers to keep
their distance.

57

Using another job offer to get a raise
in your current job is blackmail.
When you decide to go—adios
and don't look back.

58

On investing: real estate doesn't rust—
cars do. Invest in historically
good returns.

59

Don't stare at the sun or a bad golf
swing—both can be harmful.

60

Before a job interview or a client
presentation, read three industry
newsletters, one industry magazine,
talk to one employee and two customers.
You'll now know 80% of the major issues
effecting that organization.

32

61

Name your house and property;
it'll sound bigger.

62

Showing up for the interview without
a pen, notepad and questions
insults the interviewer.

63

If you're a purebred, outside sales
professional, your left shoe's sole will
wear out first from getting in and out
of the car a lot. If you're a hiring
manager, check both their souls.

33

64

When asking for advice,
seek proven counsel.

65

If you own two books,
you have a library.

If you have two apple trees,
you have an orchard.

34

If you've raised two spruce,
you have a Christmas tree farm.

If you have a tomato plant in an old
paint bucket, you're a gardener.

If you have three trees close
together, you have a forest.

If you can see the sun set,
you have a vista.

If your yard holds rainwater,
you have waterfront property.

35

If you can smell horse manure in the
morning, you're in "rare air." Savor it.

If you have a few elephants,
you have a zoo.

It's your choice that makes things so.

66

Try the R^4R_x for beginning new
actions and behaviors:

- Recognize the opportunity

- Redouble your efforts

- Recuperate and celebrate
  even small changes

- Repeat as needed in all
  facets of your life

36

67

Think of all those ten-minute bites of time you spend waiting for something or someone. What could you read, outline or organize at that moment to begin anew?

68

Apply for your passport now— spouses, too.

69

Your neighbor's income is only important if she wants to buy your house. Mind your own elephant.

70

There are others who can actually do the job better than the previous person. You did. Give others the benefit of the doubt.

71

It's not the responsibility of your employer to keep your skills fresh. It's your job to push your skill sets to a higher level.

72

Pick an employer wisely. You'll spend more waking hours at work than at home.

38

73

Never buy the last slice of pizza
from the oven at the airport
food counter. Eat fresh.

74

Don't take yourself too seriously...
nobody else does.

75

Overloading a person's voice mail
with your message is rude.
Brevity means a lot.

76

Always state your phone number when you leave a message. Don't assume.

77

"I'm sorry" goes a long way. Try it.

40

78

A good salesperson could sell a CPA a two-week timeshare starting April 1st.

79

A great salesperson could sell a widescreen TV to an Amish farmer, but wouldn't.

80

All professionals read and study the literature in their field. Hit the library or bookstore today.

81

People forget names, never smiles.

82

Always tip more than you should. Being cheap is a bad habit.

83

If you own a piano and are moving this Saturday...your friends will already have plans.

—Cheap labor wisdom

84

Stay to help clean-up after the party.

85

Stay humble: change a baby's
dirty diaper once in a while.

86

If you're gonna go to the party,
enjoy yourself.

87

Respect, honor, dignity and justice aren't
reserved for the military. They are
universal opportunities to participate.

88

If you have to "take a number" at a
bakery, ice cream store or restaurant,
it's gonna be fattening and awesome.

89

Rent *Good Will Hunting*, the original
Odd Couple, and *Wonder Boys* if your
spirit needs lifting and a fire lit under it.

90

The average adult's vocabulary
only grows 50 words a year.
Shoot for at least 200.

91

Always follow-up with a note after
an interview, business lunch or
chance meeting in the grocery
store. People remember.

92

It's total calories and exercise that
cause weight gain and weight loss.
Eat the darn donut and walk
up the stairs with a smile.

93

Send two business cards—one for them,
one to give away.

44

94

What you're willing to "give up"
tells more about you than what
you'll "stop at nothing" to get.

95

The commencement ceremony means
"the beginning."

96

Reciting the phrase "...it was meant
to be" when something turns out
badly, is a copout. Analyze what
went wrong and fix it.

97

Beep your horn under bridges when no other cars are around; it's fun and noisy.

–Kid genius

98

Go one day without complaining. And don't catch-up the next day, either.

46

99

Want to write a book? Pick a topic you know and write a pamphlet–there's your outline. For a novel: write bunches of short stories and tie them together. Or hire a professional.

100

Don't confuse activity with

47

accomplishment. Look for results.

101

Let children be children first. Love
and nurturing will keep them on track
towards maturing into a beautiful adult.

102

Remember: Loyalty and longevity
are not the same thing.

48

103

Keep some KC AND THE SUNSHINE
BAND tunes in the house. Music
is a powerful healer.

104

Accountability is the greatest gift to yourself and your friends.

105

After asking for a favor, ask, "Now, how can I help you?"

106

Love is about giving and not expecting love in return.

-Leo Buscalia

107

Sales professionals and sales managers
average less than three years with
any company they work for and get
promoted less than 25% of the time.
Consider these facts when you
interview for a job. Explore the
ranks for oldies and goodies.

108

If you *face* a purple elephant it can't kick you in the rear.

109

When times get tough in business
the urge is to re-organize. Let it go
and re-connect with customers.

110

Why does one tolerate psychological
stress or abuse for years, yet remove
a pebble in their shoe after only
a few minutes?

111

If you get to the end of your money and
still have more month left, it's time
to change something.

52

112

Chew your food not your pen cap.

113

Use optimistic language with positive first impressions. Would you buy from the guy selling for the Pompeii Life and Casualty Company?

53

114

Most people seek responsibility and praise, not authority and perks.

115

Remember your three top mentors and never forget what they taught you.

116

Remain silent and smiling when
watching a little league game.

117

Walking and running burn
close to the same amount of calories.
Walkers ponder; runners chase.
Both elements are important.

118

When starting a revolution, pack your
own lunch. Not everybody's gonna
want to go with you on your field
trip to the wild frontier.

119

Never be the "Parade Marshall"
to the buffet line at business
or social functions.

120

Prime time television is the biggest
energy zapper and time waster
in the free world.

121

Where there's coffee, so too should be
the pen. Write ideas down and act *Wow*!

122

On negotiating: most people would rather have "a little more" now than "a lot more" later.

123

Rehearse your elevator speech on any idea you're promoting. Twenty seconds—GO!

124

Your mother-in-law might be right from time to time. Just consider it.

125

Teach children along the way: manners,
hygiene, how to change a sink faucet,
toilet and garbage disposal, replace a
furnace filter, install light dimmer
switches and icemakers, how to jump
a car battery, perform CPR, build
a campfire and how to overstuff
a garbage can.

126

To save over $2000 a year, learn to
do simple home repairs or barter with
the neighbor with all the tools. Every
household should have a cordless
drill, tire pump, First Aid Kit and
a huge flashlight.

127

Never start plumbing projects after
the hardware store closes.

—Do-it-yourselfer-wisdom

128

Look carefully for the "extra" in
"ordinary" people.

58

129

Showing respect and waiting on a person
hand and foot are not the same thing.
A person deserving your respect will
not tolerate special treatment.

130

Give your boss the same book you're
reading—if you dare.

131

If you're 25-35—start to
plan activities for when you're 50.

If you're 35-45—do some of them now.

If you're 45-55—do more of them now

If you're 55-65—set an example
for the other 3 groups.

132

"Severance package" doesn't mean you can now paint the house. Let it peel, and get back to interviewing.

133

A good carpenter plays more rounds a year than a good golf club salesperson. Some jobs don't have the perks that they appear to have.

134

There's no official rule saying you have to visit relatives you don't like on the major holidays.

135

In the next 12 months read any book written by Tom Peters, Scott Peck, Ken Blanchard and a handful of Zen-to-Wow books. Life or business will never seem boring again.

136

Do something radical. Eat yogurt with chopsticks, blindfolded.

137

Job security is an illusion—unless you're a "Free Agent."

61

138

Be aware of the energy level when you
enter a home or a business.

139

We enter into marriage knowing
the odds are 50% we'll make it, yet fire
our financial planner when our
investments don't yield over 12%.
Patience works on both accounts.

140

All frustrations begin when we
realize our options.

141

Ask yourself "so what?" the next time
you think you have a big problem. See
how your thinking changes.

142

It's not the rock I fear will strike me,
but a pebble of complacency finding
its way into my shoe.

–Jonathan Grant

143

It just might be less risky to own
your own business. Would
you ever fire *yourself*?

144

Eliminate the word "worry" from
your vocabulary. It is an infecting
word that causes nasty stuff to
happen in your gut.

64

145

Ratios, cycle times, productivity,
statistical analysis and strategic
planning apply to pizza deliveries,
romantic evenings, baseball games,
thoughts and Sunday services.
Measurement leads to
success, young Jedi.

146

Would you hire you if your résumé
showed up on your desk? Make sure it
states how you solve problems, make
money or have grown business.
You'll be hired.

147

Business is what you do,
not who you are.

148

Better to make mistakes through
commission than omission.

149

If you aren't tired, don't go to bed yet.
Do something that will make a
difference tomorrow in your
job, health, finances or
personal relationships.

66

150

Your kids are watching you. They always
notice regardless of the commotion of
the party or how preoccupied
you think they are.

151

Young children don't do dumb things on purpose. Consider the discipline carefully for accidents of simply untrained judgment.

152

The first mistake a child makes in a new situation is a sign of learning.

153

Give a copy of your meeting notes to your boss. She'll depend on you the next time and time after that.

154

A "family" is not a specific gender mix or number. "Intention" creates a family.

155

It's always hip to wear a sweatshirt with your college logo.

156

Your voice should always introduce *your* voice mail. People need to know they're leaving *you* the message.

68

157

Figuring out ways to make
more money is more productive
than figuring out ways to
save more money.

158

Set New Year's resolutions in
November to ease the pressure.

159

Most things are over-determined.

–Scott Peck, MD, author

70

160

A coffee table should be judged by what
your heels say. Study the real purpose
of thoughts and things.

161

If it's illegal, report it.

162

Never plant a bush that won't even cast
a shadow. Save up to buy a bigger one.

163

To hear an echo is a worthy goal.
De-clutter.

72

164

Do STOP SIGNS ever tire of their
response? Question more of
what you see.

165

Most career choices are decided in less time than the average person spends planning a vacation to Disney World. Scary, eh? Plan, set goals, study successful people.

73

166

Never save for "retirement"
again. Replace "retirement" with
"financial independence day."
You'll save more diligently to
become financially secure
rather than waiting until...

74

167

Once a magazine is put into the
"magazine rack" it will never be
read again. Skim, read, toss.

168

It's best to tell someone when they
have gook on their nose.

169

Would Henry David Thoreau have
thought differently if he'd owned
a Harley? Would you?

170

Headhunters place less than 25% of
white-collar workers. Plan on doing the
lion's share of the work to secure a
great career track.

171

Don't expect to get the jumper cables,
four-person tent, First Aid supplies,
artificial Christmas tree, foldable lawn
chair, sleeping bag or umbrella *back* into
the original bag or "carrying case"
for "easy storage." Some things
are easier said than done.

172

Tell your significant other you love them.
Don't be so stingy with the word.

173

Everybody needs a personal advisory
board. Who's on yours?

174

Work harder on yourself than on your
job. If you work hard on your job
you'll make a living. If you work
hard on yourself, you'll
make a fortune.

–Jim Rohn

175

There is a correlation to income and
vocabulary. Learn a new word—it pays.

176

Wash your car before every client visit.
They may be looking out the window
or have you drive to lunch.

177

Once a year, take a driving vacation with
your family to reconnect with
each other and America.

178

Before you spend, ask, "What
is the return?"

179

Don't be fooled by great benefit
plans—the pay plan may stink
compared to the competitors'.
Take the money and invest
it in your own choices.

180

Long commutes will wear you down
faster than you think, regardless
of the income.

181

If no one ever leaves your
organization—watch out. The water
could be too stagnant to fish, sail
or oxygenate you adequately.

182

80

On job hunting: first call people who
have the authority to hire you.

183

Organize after five or before eight. The
meter's running the rest of the time.

184

Keep a phone log for two weeks and see just how many customers you reach.

185

Never eat a big meal before an important meeting.

186

Never have an important meeting and a big meal at the same time. Each deserves its time and place.

187

Telling the employer who just gave
you an offer that you'll "have to
talk it over with your spouse"
sounds wimpy. You probably
will–just don't admit it!

188

82

Parents and teachers communicate
accurately and regularly.

189

Never say, "I'd never do that...I could
never do that...How could you think
that?" In different circumstances
you just might!

190

Consider starting your business talk
with question & answer first–you'll get
to the core issues and the audience
feels open to speak up.

191

It's what we do when alone that builds
our character and confirms self-worth.

192

Your inner voice is your law.

193

Conflict is usually caused
by our reluctance to
deal with conflict.

84

194

Sit with your child at bedtime and count
your blessings. They will remember it
for the rest of their lives and will
grow up secure and thankful.

195

Are you really looking hard enough
at what you have to do to
make a difference?

196

Buy bagels for the group once in a while.

197

Drop a note to your doctor telling him or
her you feel great and wish them well.
Same goes for your dentist.

198

86

Pay the toll for the car behind you—live
large, spend money with flair.

199

Never say "never," and always
consider "maybe."

200

If you were a tree...would

you be proud to live

in your yard?

201

If your neighbor's basketball hoop is
bare of a net, install one on a covert
midnight mission. Cost: $3.00.
You'll smile for months.

202

Asking questions takes more energy
but adds more muscle to your
presentations and relationships.

203

Think twice before saying, "Boy, I
need a cocktail," in front of
your children or at work.

88

204

On hugs: let your child decide when
they're finished hugging you.
Don't you end it too soon.

–Peg Dahl

205

Now is a perfect time to address any
problem and seek guidance.

89

206

How much do you earn an hour?
What value can you add that
will earn you more?

207

Sending the thank you note is more
important than reciprocity.

208

Chances are, our children already have
it better than we did. Our challenge
is teaching them how to give back
to the community if they haven't
had it tough so far.

209

Reserve the word "crisis" for the real
thing. Most "crises" are really
serious, but not a crisis.

90

210

A $60.00 lesson is a better

investment than a new $300.00

graphite driver or a $250.00

racket. Deep down

you know this.

91

211

Need to think, act, write something
creative? Sit in a Starbucks coffeehouse
or bookstore to soak in the energy.

212

An expert is someone who does "it"
a lot more than you do. A child
is an expert at playing. You're
an expert at _____.

213

Better to pay an expert plumber than
pay an expert carpet cleaner too.

92

214

Explore the concepts of "manifesting"
and "synchronicity" to realize
the potential of the human
mind and spirit.

215

"Why?" tells motive. "What?" tells
reason. Ask "why?" first. Ask
deeper questions of life.

216

Zen is familiarity. Wow is opportunity.

217

First date or first interview never
ask, "Want to see my tattoo?"
Read thy audience.

218

Keep a journal on your nightstand:
It's easier to fall asleep having written
down what you want to remember.

219

Buy a vacation souvenir,
no matter how small.

94

220

Take full accountability for
your actions and thoughts.
No excuses.

95

221

Aphorisms are easier written
than executed.

222

Don't envy the silver spoon.
Homemade ones of wood don't tarnish.

223

Before you give up on anything, have
you *really* given it your all and
examined every option?

96

224

What you profess to be "loyalty"
sometimes disguises itself
as fear of change.

97

225

Your revolution doesn't have to be
really big–just meaningful.

226

98

Entrepreneurs started saving their lunch money for their voyage long before you saw them set sail. Start socking some bucks away for your sailboat.

227

"Is what I'm ***about*** to do going to
take me closer to or further from
my goal?" A tough question
to ask yourself 25 times a day.
(This question's worth repeating.)

228

When someone yells "HEADS UP!", don't.

Just duck.

229

Done reading this book? Back to work
or studying then. "Luck favors the
prepared mind," they say.

230

Cultivate an attitude of gratitude.

231

Give thanks.

232

Want to have a productive
and creative business meeting or
family discussion? Why not use
the Zen-to-Wow mindset? Simply
have everybody read the book
and bring three ideas to the
table. Start talking about
how to WOW. Repeat as
needed for success.

Now it's your turn...

Rob Engelman, President of Engelman Management Group, provides marketing and management leadership through contract consulting and "best practices" seminars to companies ranging from start-ups to Fortune 100 behemoths. Organizations such as Citicorp, McDonald's Corporation, and the Chicago Bar Association have benefited from Rob's unique brand of strategic thought leadership and nationally acclaimed training programs including *Best Practices of Personal Marketing*, *SUREFIRE Marketing*, and *Negotiations Made Simple*.

In addition to being a writer on current business issues and a trusted, quoted expert in national publications, Rob is an adjunct instructor at the University of Chicago - Graham School of General Studies, as well as other leading universities.

Rob holds an MBA from Northwestern University's Kellogg School of Management, a BA from Dartmouth College, and a Certificate in Management and Leadership from the University of Michigan Business School. He is also an active member of TEC International.

A die-hard Cubs fan, avid tennis player, and skier, Rob lives in the northern suburbs of Chicago with his wife, two children, two frogs, and a few purple elephants roaming the yard.

He can be reached at 847-945-7573 or via e-mail at **rob@engelmanmanagement.com**.

Russ Riendeau, PhD, is an internationally recognized author and speaker on motivation and peak performance in sales and management. A behavioral scientist by education, he's also senior partner of The East Wing Search Group, an executive search firm located in Barrington, Illinois, which specializes in management, marketing and sales search.

Russ has interviewed over 52,000 business professionals since 1985, sharing his research in three previous books, *Finders Keepers: Attracting and Retaining Top Sales Professionals*, *The Insider's Guide to Getting Great Job Offers* (co-authored with Brady Spencer), and *Thinking On Your Seat*, articles and appearances in *The Wall Street Journal, Chicago Tribune*, TEC International, and TV/radio appearances.

Holding a doctorate in developmental psychology from Capella University in Minneapolis, a MA in psychology and a BA in applied behavioral sciences from National-Louis University, in Chicago, Russ is also a pilot, distance runner, cyclist, hockey player and coach. His family lives on Blue Heron Pond with their own herd of purple elephants, just west of Paris, France, in Barrington, Illinois. He can be reached at 847-381-0977 or at **www.russellriendeau.com**.